WAITING FOR PIPPA TO PURRRRRR

by Stacia Ferguson

Illustrations by Mark Watts

Waiting for Pippa to Purrr Copyright 2019©Stacia Ferguson

All rights reserved. No part of this book may be reproduced or transmitted in any form or by any means, electronic or mechanical, including photocopying, recording, or by an information storage and retrieval system—except by a reviewer who may quote brief passages in a magazine, newspaper, or online review—without permission in writing from the publisher.

A PURRR PUBLICATIONS BOOK

Contact the author: staciaferguson@purrrpublications.com
Visit the artist's website: airwatts.net

Thank you...

For those who rescue rescues and in turn, themselves are rescued.

I would also like to give a shout-out to Mom and Dad, my soul sister Andriana Todorova, my illustrator Mark and his parents Valencia and Joseph Watts. And William Armitage who is the bee's knees.

I want to give the biggest shout-out to my rescued doggie Pippa. Pippa has opened my heart and mind to Imagination and Possibilities.

"Hi, my name is Daisy and I'm five years old."

"Ooops, I mean five."

"I have two pets."

"This is my cat Trisket."

"This is my doggie Pippa."

"I know

Pippa and Trisket

are the same

in every way."

"Mommy, mommy. I have a question...why doesn't Pippa purr?"

"Sorry Daisy-Roo,
But Pippa is a doggie and doggies don't purr."

However, Daisy-Roo, I do think Pippa purrs to you in different ways.

"...like the times Pippa...

...protects and encourages me."

"Or when I sometimes don't want to eat all my veggies…"

"...Pippa helps me

gobble them up."

"Pippa lets me dress her up in silly girly outfits."

Having fun with Pippa, sometimes we make a mess.

But being PUT
in the corner makes
fun much less.

"Pippa prepares me for for a perfect day."

"Pippa takes my nervous nerves away."

"Pippa greets me at the door with a big..."

Hooray!

"Then we sleePURRR the night away…"

THE END